DINNER WITH SUPERMAN

ALSO BY JANE BONNYMAN

An Ember from the Fire (Poetry Salzburg, 2016)

DINNER WITH SUPERMAN

Poems

Jane Bonnyman

RED SQUIRREL PRESS

First published in 2020 by Red Squirrel Press
36 Elphinstone Crescent
Biggar
South Lanarkshire
ML12 6GU
www.redsquirrelpress.com

Typeset and designed by Gerry Cambridge
e: gerrycambridge@btinternet.com

Cover art: Jane Bonnyman

A CIP catalogue record for this book is available from
the British Library.

ISBN: 978 1 910437 98 8

Red Squirrel Press is committed to a sustainable future.
This book is printed in Scotland by Love & Humphries
Using Forest Stewardship Council certified paper.
www.loveandprint.co.uk

Contents

'Lord, what fools these mortals be!'

A Midsummer Night's Dream

Spider-Man: The Final Chapter

When I think of the times you were late, hurling your bike against a railing,
swinging into the café two minutes before closing, still hoping for dinner,
and how one slow morning, you told me your job would always come first—
such is the matter of saving lives—long days and consecutive nights;

it takes me back to our second date when you shrugged off your jumper
to reveal your favourite t-shirt with the giant tarantula drawn on the front.
I screamed because it was bigger than your head, and in the evening light
its legs seemed to move across your chest. *Got it in Australia*, you said.

And even then, I could picture the comic scene: you in the webbed-mask
and Spandex suit, whisking me between two buildings and up to the stars—
everything hinging on the hero with the fashion sense and superpowers—
and the final shot: the two of us, above the neon city, hanging by a thread.

Wasteland

We left the pink glow of the Persian Café,
the lemon strip of the hotel,
and strayed into an unlit street.
It ought to be there in the curve of dark,
where we would turn away and end it.
Houses loomed behind fir trees,
abandoned sheds crouched
in corners like sleeping bears,
and pathways unfurled with steps out of sync,
mud-covered hearth stones, bits of brick.

Once by the lamppost,
you said the first words all night:
Could I explain again why... but how could I
in the middle of a cul-de-sac,
among forgotten sandbags, bent railings,
windscreen glass, tell you it was the fear
of being too long in this place,
lingering like ghost moths,
beneath a single light in the wasteland,
breathing rust grains from the wind?

La P'tite Folie

When, on our blind date in the French restaurant,
while you're telling me about your six-day hike
through the wilderness of the Southern Alps,
I lean towards you and set fire to my hair,
accidently dipping it into the candle flame,

you watch as if it were happening on a screen:
me clutching a damp napkin to my head,
sweeping the singed strands from the tablecloth,
apologising for the mess. Somewhere Piaf sings
Non, je ne regrette rien, and you ask for the bill.

And I think I always knew, the way some things
seem to be meant, that it would end like this:
one half-eaten soufflé, me working out the tip,
and the chill from the open door as you,
already in your coat, run for the hills.

Munro-Lover

Bleary-eyed, in the hall cupboard,
you rummage for your Crusader rucksack,
Gore-Tex fleece. By dawn you're trekking
through heather, blanket bog, moss,
heart drumming in your ears.
Soon you will hold the world
in an outstretched glove.
The uncanny stillness.

Cloud shadows drift over the loch,
Sunlight spills across the dark,
and you think you know something of love:
the thrill of courtship, the life-long pairing,
eyries scattered across the home range:
Vorlich. Schiehallion. More. Vane.

Director

When we hug goodbye, he says
Lips and we kiss. It's perfunctory,
like reaching up to dust the light
or water the plant on the dresser.

I'd met him before, once, to discuss
education, resourcing, council funding,
but now we're standing on the platform,
while folk wheel past cases and lug children.

He has to go. Glasgow by four. Emails to send.
He leans in again. I break away, telling him
I have to get shoes. We speak about shoes.
He stares at his brogues. Top quality.
So bloody comfy—got them in Italy.

For God's sake just get on the train.

Weather Man

Not those months spent
in Texas and New Orleans,
studying the impact of a hurricane,
or the time you scaled the inside
of a wind turbine to fix a cable
and measure the blade rotation,
or the tornado you chased
in an act of derring-do
across the Great Plains;

rather it was the night
when you stopped by a shop window
on the way to the restaurant
to check out your hair, your scarf,
the lie of your coat and muttered
Lookin' good... under your breath—
that image of you, there, beside me
winking and hi-fiving the glass
was what really blew me away.

Dinner with Superman

For a good hour I've been studying him—
the polished brogues, designer jeans,
the crisp white shirt, the gleaming teeth
of that all-American smile. I think I love him:
the foal-brown of his eyes; the touch of his skin
when he reaches for the bill. *I'll get this,* he says.
His voice is like a breeze, drifting through timothy
in a far-off prairie. He asks to walk me home
and once outside, I notice his height—
so tall his head brushes the lining of clouds.
He leans against a side of tenement,
looks around for his date. *Goodbye,* he says,
glancing down, *I've got an early morning flight.*
I stand in front of my door like a Lego woman,
my arm raised in the posture of a wave.
In the distance the red flash of a cape.

Stuntman

So used to performing feats
known only to Spiderman,
or those on impossible missions,
his conversation is minimal.

He's always lost in thoughts
of trapdoors, elevator shafts, revolving walls,
never looks me in the eye,
preferring the sideways glance
to weigh up danger.

There have been past escapes:
leaping from trains, supermarkets,
shimmying out of bus shelters,
hiding within layers of jumpers.

One night he asks me for a lift,
and while the car waits at the lights,
I tell him about my life.
We listen to the indicator ticking,
the arrow signalling *left, left.*

It might need a few takes
to capture the seat belt's arc in mid-air,
the way one hand scoops up
his laptop, bag and coffee cup,
while he kicks open the door.

In a whirlwind I hardly register,
he vanishes into night streets,
and I won't see him again,
unless there's a chance meeting
on a plane, or at a poetry reading.

Writer

After he told me
that once in a pavement café
in the Place de la Bastille
when, in conversation with friends,
he threw his head back to laugh,
and a pigeon shat in his mouth,
I could not kiss him.

He wrote poetry with French words,
said my eyes glinted like malachite.

It didn't work.
I just thought he was full of it.

La La Land

You take my hand
and we step onto the road,
my heels echo on the cobbles
as we swing past townhouses,
box hedges, BMW convertibles.
You're wearing a velvet jacket
a starched shirt and scarlet bow tie.
I'm in rose chiffon, ivory brocade,
tiny pearls scattered in my hair.
Somewhere an orchestra crescendos,
and you throw me into the air.
I glide over rooftops, the tennis club,
and spin lighter than a sycamore key
into your arms. Our eyes meet.
You lean in. A voice shouts *Cut!*

And we're outside the pub,
you're buttoning your coat,
saying thanks for a lovely evening,
but you'd better get your train.
I set off alone, being sure to ignore
the moon and all those stars—
silver coins sent into the dark,
printed with imagined scenes
like the one when you walk me home
through Ann Street, at midnight,
where the globe lights are lemon drops
and the pavement's bathed in gold.
You turn to me and smile.
I whisper, *Is this La La Land?*
Then you ask me to dance.

The Look of Love

Would you like Dusty or Nat King Cole? you ask,
and I realise the line's rehearsed—
you've spent the afternoon laying out, in order,
the hits you hoped I'd like,
and suddenly the bowl of potato salad,
the red wine on the shelf,
the two cat mugs next to the kettle give you away,
and I'm sitting in a room where flowers,
scatter cushions, the positioning of chairs
are waiting for an unwritten scene,
and if I turned on my heels they would grow tiny legs,
like the dish and the spoon, and chase me
into the night calling *Don't go! Don't ever go!*

An Evening with Hugh

after A Far Cry from Kensington *by Muriel Spark*

He talks about the golf club, a career for his daughter.
His neck is thicker than she remembers.
After the oysters, he flops his hand onto hers
and says she's *very understanding,*
which makes her think of mothers, kind aunts, do-gooding.
She prods the salmon mousse with her fork,
sips the Sauvignon she doesn't like.
Later in the marble bathroom she considers slipping out
in search of another evening—

perhaps a garden, at midnight, lit by a bright moon,
borders of pansies, hollyhocks, marigolds,
and him, waiting on the silver lawn.
Someone turns the radio on. He pulls her close
and whirls her round and round.
Their laughter drifts over sleeping houses
and the big band plays. Is that 'Sunshine Serenade'
or 'Sugar Blues'? How long will they dance?
Here's Artie Shaw with 'Stardust.'

In Your Favourite Café

I snuck in here
when I wasn't looking,
found myself sitting
by the window, staring
at crumbling paint,
the letters spelling
COFFEE back to front.

I see you in the empty chair,
picking at the icing
on your Empire biscuit.
Milky foam clings
to the sides of your cup.
You wear your old glasses,
your navy coat, a jumper
I think I bought for you.

It's when I almost hear
the familiar rhythms of your voice,
I realise I'm waiting on the past
to tell me something—
the thing I didn't quite get—
but I pick up my bag,
am through the glass door
and onto the street,
before you know I was there.

Dream Sequence

Which brings me back to your tenement.
Stone steps. Stained glass. Wild geraniums.
A green bike tied to the bannister.
A canoe propped against the wall.
Tall windows thrown open
to the December night.

You're on the fifth floor,
pulling her close, whispering into her ear.
A photo frame faces down on the piano.
I give up on the stairs and summon a ladder,
like the one that might descend from a UFO.
A close-up of my fingers, grasping the metal rung.

Now you're in the bedroom, pulling clothes
from drawers, piling jumpers into a case.
I want to go to you,
but there's a black storm door.
My eye moves to the keyhole,
and the whole flat's on fire.

White flames swallow the hat-stand.
A helicopter lands in the hall.
And before you take off through the roof,
you ask me what I'm doing there.
My casual answers. *Just passing.*
Came to return the key. Saw your light was on.

A Date with Farmer Oak

He can predict the weather by a slight shift in cloud,
a toad slumped in the doorway, a rook's uneasy call.

He traces his thumb along the jawbone of a skull,
half-buried in heather, and pronounces it 'hare',

then points out a lapwing, a buzzard feather,
star flowers, bog myrtle, unusual rock formations.

He walks for hours without water, slings his tired dog
onto his shoulder as if it were a new born lamb.

Later, during dinner, I ask about life in Dorset,
his father, his love of folk music; but he won't answer.

Instead, he slices a clean line through his burger,
and pierces each chip exactly in the centre.

Once finished, he looks up and tells me
he's sorry but he doesn't eat and talk.

It's ok, I reply, *there's a silence that says much.*
Outside, the sky grows darker than oil cloth.

He leaves without pudding.
He must see to the barley and wheatstacks.

From the window, I watch him stride away from me
in his waxed jacket, collar up against the wind.

Ed. Fairfax_1

I'm difficult to sum up:

expert communicator—across vast distances—
who loves to travel (Spanish Town, Paris, Rome),
throws great parties, is comfortable financially,
has a strong baritone voice and a penchant for duets,
tries to keep fit, often escapes to the country,
can identify most species of flower, moth, dragonfly.

Bad points—*what the deuce!*—I don't have many:
the odd mood swing, a few skeletons in the closet.
I like to smoke cigars on midsummer evenings,
when their scent blends with rose, southernwood.

Looking for someone good, amusing, into reading
and brooding heroes. She must have a certain idealism,
take me out of myself, be skilled in French and firefighting,
believe in me when others have written me off,
and never look at me coldly for promising her
the life of her dreams, then snatching it away.

She mustn't blame me if she's still there
after the closing scene, waiting, as the credits roll,
for some door into another world. She'll be used
to staring into sunsets, pinpointing each moment
of weakening light, and she'll know, like any other Jane,
how even the most brilliant rainbow fades back to air.

Undateable

half a jar
of tomato sugo
in the fridge door
cherry red
after so many months

sits beside
the mustard pot
with a stuck lid
sprouted garlic
a white lemon

No Place Like Home

You want it to open on a technicolour scene. Picture Dorothy
after the storm, leaving her farmhouse, those lace curtains, cloth quilts.
After Toto's landing yelp, you hear singing starting up and twist the key,
but it snaps, the brass tip held by the closed door, the way some men
don't give back the last piece of your heart. You hold the cool stalk,
the pink bird keyring still intact, and wonder how you managed it.

Later, in the kitchen, you're afraid of thought: what if the only light
you'll ever see is window-light, and the winter moon will watch you
from the cupola as you shift from room to room, dusting, tidying?
Occasionally, folk will post through cards, 10" pizzas, items in flat pack.
They'll keep it up for a bit, but soon, they'll forget. With money running out,
only candles, dried spaghetti tucked in a corner, a raisin in the bottom of a bag.

You'll live for the atlas under the bed, imagine San Salvador, Honolulu,
smell hibiscus, jasmine, the ocean. That's you striding away from yourself
on the Rue Saint-Antoine, or sitting in a Manhattan apartment next to
a piano, as if you'd just written a greatest hit, versus the you now flopped
on the sofa while the cat paws a bluebottle to the floor, crunches its wings.
The clock ticks loudly above the sink. You're considering digging out

photographs, reloading Netflix, when you hear his voice echo through the hall.
Has he come to tell you he wishes things were different, that he wants more
than your poetry-readings on the porch or your paper aeroplane notes?
Has he decided he's fed up of you stuck behind four walls? Or *Is it finally
him?* you whisper to the transparent animals in the cabinet under the stair,
the gentleman caller, apologising for being late. He says he'll have to replace

the lock, that it'll cost. Both of you crouch down either side of the letterbox. You stare into his eyes, thinking he might be the one to set you on the ribbon that spirals into your dreams, to rewrite those discarded songs, buy you Martinis on the beach. No! Stop! He doesn't exist. Like Batman, Zorro, a frog-turned-
    prince,
he's just another wizard, speaking from behind a screen, dazzling you with flames and special effects, while the sparkling city, quieter than breath, sinks into sand.

Dear Alasdair

If, on the trip I never made to Oxford, I chance
upon you in the languages section of Blackwell's,
while scanning the spines for your latest book:
Proust: The Life, In Search of Lost Time Explained,
or, one autumn evening, as light slips
from the scene, I run into you in Bloomsbury,
hugging a flute of irises to your coat;

or by some twist of fate, I end up next you
on the 13.13. to Paris, and you glance at me
in between writing an essay on Villon,
and speaking on the phone to Céline,
who has missed you and is cooking lamb
and tarte tatin to go with the Bordeaux St Julien
you'll pick up on your way home;

if we meet again, I'd like to tell you
that you won't know who I am, except
as a picture that flickers across a screen,
the way I imagine each version of you
wheeling into life like characters on a zoetrope
until it's hard to remember the you I met
so long ago, that July in Edinburgh
when, for a moment, the world tilted
and veered from its usual course.

What was the sound of your voice?
And your eyes—were they garnet brown
or a darker quartz?

P.S. I hope you never read this.

What's For You

Saturday. The A39 is gridlocked. Should've set off earlier.
Too busy dreaming, loading the car, recording the mixtape.
Two hours later we're singing *I've had the time of my life*
and *I will survive* on a single carriageway from Tavistock.

No one's bought tickets in advance, hoping their degrees
in Physics, Economics, French, or that gym membership
might stand a chance. At the last pit stop, I mention
baggage. Is it too much? And the levels of neurosis

between us? The light's fading when we reach the coast.
Seagulls bigger than dogs loom as we prod wooden forks
into chips and study the clean horizon. Finally, someone
states the obvious, and the huge sea rolls in and out.

We head to the beach. Swig the traditional gin. And build
a fire with driftwood, crates, an abandoned front door.
Together in a circle we turn back the clock and remember
a fleet of them sailing past. Here's to luck, to happenstance!

It's late. We should make a move. There's always next year.
On the way home to our lives, I whisper my mother's words:
What's for you, won't go by you. And the road winds into the dark.
Ahead, only the midnight sky and its endless capacity for stars.

'Hope is the thing with feathers' /
(Emily Dickinson attends a 'Badminton Meetup')

Among the badminton club's finest amateurs—
who tell me to *Move! Move! Hit it straight!*
Stand closer to the net! and *Get back! Back!*—
I find you, quietly passing me the shuttlecock,
balanced on your racket like a crown for Krishna,
saying *Your shot* with a smile that understands
humiliation: the faded sportswear, fake enthusiasm.
Perhaps you're not interested in the competition?

The woman opposite in the wristbands and visor
adopts a dramatic 'ready position'. Her partner,
fitter than an Olympian, paces the tramlines.
The tension is palpable. I whack it. Then *Whoosh!*
A swift darts to the rafters. And I feel a certain delight,
watching it soar above us all. At least in the effort.
As a mark of commitment. Even if the damn thing
lands in a kit bag, or (fatally) in someone else's court.

Diva Poem

No more 'Little Miss Fearful', 'Little Miss Shy'.
One spin routine and she's ripped the bars
from the cell. Now she stands in the dawn light,
arms akimbo, gold boobs, tiara, blue satin pants,
ready for arch villains and infantry fighting tanks.

It's a wonder, when you think of the quiet girl
hiding behind the desk in the twin set and pearls.
Great Aphrodite! Great Hera! Merciful Minerva!
(We didn't know she had it in her!) The men she saves
from burning planes, submarines, warehouse rooftops!

Perhaps, given enough airtime and comic book pizzazz
you too could whip off the thick vintage specs, shed
the tiny meeping self and don some badass boots.
Finally—after all this time—a true Amazonian.
Let's call you She-Ra, Boudicca or G I Jane!

Thank Hippolyta, your life will never be the same,
as, even without the gifts from the gods—the sword,
the winged horse and those indestructible bracelets—
you'll break free from all chains, stride to the front
with a smile that says *Shazam! I am what I am!*

Rewriting The Notebook

You've never climbed a Ferris wheel
to woo me with some daring stunt,
or restored a plantation house, spending
nights pinned to a ladder, painting blue
for the shutters, white for the front.

You didn't row me into a forest lake,
easing the boat through continents
of goslings that scattered like dreams
when a heaven-splitting storm brought
rain so heavy we couldn't breathe.

You won't play dead under traffic lights,
waiting for the screech of a touring truck,
or pick fights with my bourgeois father.
You don't snap or yell or slap
the car door, letting me drive off alone.

You are the man who walks me home.
In the darkest hours. In Siberian snow.
I don't need to ask. You're always there.
No fury or hubbub, yours is a quiet love,
but it's enough, it's enough.

Late

The sound of the radio,
water spilling into the bath,
the hush of traffic on Gibson Street.

Warm air from the open window,
the apricot sky and the hill's shadow,
lit squares from the tenements opposite.

I ease myself into blue water.
My toe brushes the rim of tea-light.

You watch me from the doorway,
two giant towels in your arms.

Acknowledgements

Some of these poems have appeared in the following publications: *Magma, Obsessed with Pipework, Sogo Magazine* and *The Dark Horse.*

'Dinner with Superman', 'In Your Favourite Café,' and 'Munro-Lover' first appeared in *House of Three: Volume 1*, published by Hybrid Press, 2016.

With many thanks to Gerry Cambridge, Gerrie Fellows, Jane McKie and Sheila Wakefield.

A NOTE ON THE TYPE

This pamphlet is set in Centaur, now considered a classic serif typeface, originally designed by American book and type designer Bruce Rogers for the Metropolitan Museum of Art in New York in 1914. With a beauty that sacrifices nothing to readability, its functional elegance makes it an excellent choice for the setting of poetry.